Tarsi,
the Sandhill Crane

Tarsi,
the Sandhill Crane

by

Liz Drewien Thach

Illustrated by Vivian Olsen

To Zia, Liam and Callia

Copyright © 2010 by Liz Drewien Thach
ISBN: 1453692061
EAN-13: 9781453692066

PUBLISHER:
KATHLEEN TOSH BOOKS
4322 Oakridge
Penngrove, California 94951
USA

Visit our website at: _www.kathleentoshbooks.wordpress.com_
Email: _lizthach@aol.com_

First Kathleen Tosh Books paperback printing: July 2010
Printed in the United States of America

Contents

CHAPTER ONE

The Homecoming

He came to us in the pocket of a shirt -
my Dad's shirt. Mom, Celeste and I were in the
kitchen making dinner and setting the table and
Michelle was in the living room playing with a
puzzle when my father walked in the backdoor
that day.

"Hi, I'm home," he said grinning. "Notice
anything different about me?"

We all turned to look at him, but he seemed
the same as always. His face was suntanned from
many hours outdoors, his hair was windswept and
he was smiling as usual. Then suddenly something began to wiggle in the pocket of his green
and blue plaid shirt, and a small, brown head

popped out and looked at us with curious red-brown eyes.

"Peep," it said.

"Oh, a bird," squealed Michelle, as she ran into the kitchen from the living room. "Can we see him?"

Dad gently lifted the small fuzzy creature from his pocket and placed him in the palm of his hand. The bird was so small that he fit perfectly.

On closer inspection, we could see that he was covered with a soft cinnamon down like a baby chicken, and when we touched him timidly, he felt like velvet. His eyes were a glowing brown and his tiny beak was pink, but the most unusual thing about him was his long legs. They were twice the length of his body, and folded in two beneath him. Salmon-pink in color and rubbery to the touch, his legs bent inwards at the knees, as do all bird legs, but to Celeste, Michelle and I this was fascinating as we felt his knees were so unique compared to ordinary human knees.

"He's a baby Greater Sandhill Crane," said Dad, the biologist.

"A baby crane," we said with awe, "can we keep him?"

"Yes, we're going to raise him, because he's an orphan. I found him in the marsh today all alone and lost when I went to check the nests of the other cranes."

We had moved to Grays Lake, Idaho several months ago so Dad could study the Greater Sandhill Cranes. Even though it was called Grays Lake, it was really a large marsh covered with bulrush and cattails. But the marsh was home to hundreds of Greater Sandhills which migrated here each summer from New Mexico, Arizona, and Old Mexico to nest and raise their young.

"Wow, look at his feet," exclaimed Celeste. "His toenails are so sharp."

Celeste was eight-years old with a round freckled face surrounded by curly blonde hair. She was always noticing details about bugs, plants, and animals and professed that she wanted to be a scientist like Dad.

"And he's got three toes," chimed in Michelle.

Michelle was the baby. She was only five and everyone treated her special because they said she was so cute. To Celeste and I, she didn't seem that cute, but I guess her big eyes, bright smile, and wispy curls of smoky brown hair appealed to grown-ups.

In an effort to establish my credibility as the eldest - ten years old - and therefore the smartest, I pointed to the part of his leg between knee and foot and announced, "These are called tarsals."

"Very good, Liz," said my Dad. "That part of his leg is called a tarsal, and it is very important to a crane. As he grows older, he will use his legs as a key means of defense against predators."

Looking at legs, we realized that they would grow much longer as he grew older. And his toe-nails, which were now very tiny and sharp, would

grown hard and strong so that he could fight
off coyotes by lashing out his legs and nails as a
weapon.

"What shall we call him?" asked Celeste.

"Well, since his tarsals are so important to
him, why don't we call him Tarsi," said Dad.

"Yes, yes," we chorused. "Tarsi, the Sandhill Crane from Grays Lake, Idaho."

So Tarsi came to our house to live. The
house was quite small, but it didn't seem to matter
to him. He lived in a cardboard box that Mom
found for him. It was filled with soft, old blankets and a heat lamp to keep him warm at night.
During the day, he was allowed to wander around
the house on his long wobbly crane legs.

We would follow him to make sure he
didn't get lost, but since the house only had three
rooms, it was difficult for him to get lost. We had

moved from the University of Idaho to spend the spring, summer, and fall months at Grays Lake so Dad could do his research on the cranes. But the only place for us to live was the Forest Service Ranger Station, which was located next to the Grays Lake National Wildlife Refuge. Unfortunately it did not come with the standard features.

Mom grimaced the first time she had a chance to explore it completely.

"Ugh, we're going to have to pump all of our water from a well", she pointed towards a red pump that was located several yards from the house, "and carry it into the house in buckets."

And sure enough, we had to take turns pumping the handle of the red pump to push the icy cold water, into an old metal bucket, and then carry it into the house to heat on the stove.

The stove was also a reason for dismay according to my mother. "I can't believe we have to live in a house with only a wood-burning stove!"

Each evening Dad would go out to the round woodshed that was located near the barn and chop wood into small pieces to light a fire in the stove. Once the stove was hot, we could then heat water and cook, as well as warm up the house, since the stove was also the only source of heat.

But despite the hardships of the Ranger

Station, Tarsi, Celeste, Michelle, and I enjoyed ourselves. Grays Lake Valley was a beautiful place to spend the summer. The nine-mile long marsh, which was situated in the center of the valley, was surrounded by tall mountains covered with quaking aspen, Douglas fir, and lodge-pole pine trees. On the foothills and flatlands above the marsh, were ranches that had been homesteaded by the kind people who had inhabited the valley for over one hundred years. The nearest town, Soda Springs, was forty-five miles away, but the valley had a small store with a post office, named Wayan.

As the summer days passed, Tarsi grew quickly and his appetite was endless. We fed him hard-boiled eggs, soft dog food, mosquitoes, and other insects. When he was being fed he always purred happily in a humming "carrrooo" sound. Afterwards he went to sleep in his box, or sometimes he'd cuddle happily on someone's lap and even try to walk up their chest and snuggle his beak in their hair. The first time he did this to me, I was quite surprised.

"What is he doing?" I whispered loudly to Mom, as Tarsi tried to put his beak in my hair and go to sleep on my neck.

"He probably thinks you're his mother," smiled Mom, "and your hair probably feels similar to feathers."

Tarsi settled down to sleep on my chest then with his head snuggled up in my hair and began

to make soft purring sounds similar to a kitten. His beak tickled my neck, but it still felt nice. Many evenings after that we took turns snuggling Tarsi, and then placing him gently in his box so he could go to sleep on his soft blankets.

Within three weeks, Tarsi grew from a palm-sized chick of six inches to a full twelve inches tall. Soon he was walking around the house, curious about everything. He'd peck at the bottom of chairs, yank at Mom's throw rugs, and try to steal the game pieces when we played Monopoly on the floor.

One day when Celeste and I returned to the house from playing ball and Michelle was outside planting flowers with Mom, we went to Tarsi's box to let him out so we could play with him. But Tarsi's box was empty, and after looking around the room, we couldn't find him.

Celeste ran out the front door, letting the screen door slam behind her. "Mom, where is Tarsi?" she yelled from the front porch.

Mom and Michelle looked up from planting holly-hocks. "Why he's in his box isn't he?" answered Mom.

"No, he isn't," I said, coming to stand by Celeste.

"Oh no," she answered worriedly, wiping her hands on her jeans as she stood up quickly. "Let's go look for him."

So we all went back into the house and searched for him. We called his name and talked to him in crane-talk.

"Carroo, carroo," we called. Suddenly we heard a loud peeping sound coming from the bedroom. We ran there, but still could not see him.

"Tarsi, Tarsi," we cried.

"Peep, peep," was the response.

Finally Michelle yelled, "I found him," and we rushed over to the bed where she was kneeling. Michelle lifted the side of the patchwork quilt, and there, peeping frantically in the dark and trapped by the enveloping bed covers, was Tarsi.

He rushed out, "carrooing" loudly, and was clearly very pleased to see us.

We petted him and held him, and Mom laughed.

"Well, I guess he's big enough to climb out of his box on his own now. Looks like Tarsi is really growing up."

And sure enough, within the next few weeks - less than six weeks after he was hatched - he was two feet tall!

His feathers were still cinnamon in color, but his legs were longer and starting to turn a darker, grey-black color. His beak was also growing bigger. Mom agreed that since he was so much larger, and appeared to be self-sufficient, that he could be allowed to roam around the house at will

and stay outside if accompanied by us.

Tarsi enjoyed being outside in the warm summer sun. He would hide in the lilac bushes that surrounded the sides of the house, or stand underneath the tall spruce trees that lined both the front and the back of the Ranger Station as a wind-break.

Inside the house, he wandered around freely, obviously quite at home in the three rooms. He had gotten tall enough to steal food off the table while we were eating, if we didn't watch him.

"Mom," yelled Michelle one morning. "Tarsi just stole my pancake."

"What?" shrieked Mom.

"See there he goes again."

And sure enough, Tarsi's quick beak was reaching onto Michelle's plate in another attempt to steal a small pancake.

"Make him stop," said Mom. "He needs to learn better manners."

So we told Tarsi he couldn't eat from the table, but every once in a while, we would slip a scrap of food to him. He was still allowed to stay in the kitchen and watch while we were eating - even though, no beaks were allowed on the table.

There was another problem with Tarsi wandering around the house, and that was the biological fact that most birds leave numerous piles of droppings behind each day. Tarsi was no exception - and he was growing larger with each passing week. It was interesting to note how the size of the piles were in direct ratio to the new inch Tarsi would grow each week. Mom soon had to set up a Tarsi-pile-cleaning-routine, which meant that each of us had to take turns cleaning up Tarsi's little natural gifts.

"Who's turn is it this time?" she would yell.

"Michelle's, Celeste's, Liz's" was the contradictory cry.

And there were often small fights over whose turn it was next to clean up a pile, but after awhile, Tarsi became house-trained, and it was no longer a problem.

Instead he would stand next to the back door and peck on the metal door screen until one of us would let him out. He would used the same method to summon us when he wanted back in; rapidly tapping his beck on the outside of the screen door while peering in at us with his lively brown eyes.

After six weeks, we realized that Tarsi always stayed near the house when he was outside and didn't wander off. So we experimented, a little at a time, to see if he would be safe on his own.

One day while we were playing in the yard with him, a large black dog from the neighbor's ranch came running into the yard. The dog ran straight for Tarsi and we screamed and yelled at the dog, but all of a sudden, Tarsi spread out his wings in a four-feet wingspan and leaning forward on his toes, hissed loudly at the dog. Then to our surprise, he rushed forward to attack the

dog. The black dog looked startled and turned to run, but Tarsi rushed forward and pecked the dog in the behind. The dog fled from the yard yelping.

After that, we knew that Tarsi would be safe on his own at night. We rarely had visitors, since the valley was so far from any cities, and we now knew we didn't have to worry about dogs.

So the summer moved along, and Tarsi grew rapidly. His legs and beak turned black, and grey feathers began to show among the cinnamon. His wings got longer, and he was able to move and run quite fast.

In the evenings after dinner, the whole family, including Tarsi, would go outside and sit on the front porch watching the sunset. There was no television to watch or telephone to answer, so this became the custom.

The sunset in itself was quite a show - long streams of orange and pink highlighting the western sky. The marsh was in front of the house, and we could hear the wild Greater Sandhill cranes calling to one another as the sun set. "Carroo, carroo," they would call in their deep, bugle-like, adult voices. The sounds echoed around the valley, bouncing off the large dark mountains silhouetted on the horizon. And Tarsi would purr contentedly next to us as we all watched the colors fade and the dark night take over the sky, the first stars twinkling in the distance.

CHAPTER TWO

Rituals

Before long, Tarsi became a very important friend and companion for Celeste, Michelle and me. Together we set up daily rituals which filled the summer with fun and delight.

A key ritual was the morning outhouse run and dance. As the three-room Ranger Station was not equipped with running water, we would rise from our beds and dashing outside in our long cotton nightgowns, skip towards the outhouse which was about fifty yards away. Tarsi was now spending the nights sleeping next to the row of tall spruce trees behind the house, and as soon as he saw us open the back screen door, he would jump out from the trees and flap his wings in greeting. Then it was off to the outhouse in a race to see who would get there first.

Tarsi always won the race. He was faster than us on his long black legs, and he had the unfair advantage of using his wings to help propel him. And there he would stand, next to the outhouse door, waiting for us to arrive.

When we got there Celeste, Michelle, and I would take turns going in while the other two waited outside with Tarsi - but then the game really began, because whoever entered the outhouse first and shut the door was sure to see a long black beak poking itself through a crack in the door. This was Tarsi's delight - to stick his beak in the crack and, glaring with one brown eye, dare the person on the wooden bench to come out. This always would illicit giggles and screams of mock fear from whomever was occupying the outhouse throne.

Switching places in the outhouse took real skill, because as soon as we tried to exit the outhouse, Tarsi's next trick was a playful attempt to

peck us in the backside. This got to be a game of dexterity, as I would leave the outhouse, hold the door open for Celeste or Michelle and attempt to slip out of Tarsi's pecking range. Celeste and Michelle always howled in triumph if Tarsi got me, but soon we all became quite good at side-stepping him.

The next ritual, after the outhouse, was the morning dance. This always occurred in the large space in front of the outhouse, woodshed and barn. It was a large patch of dirt and scraggly grass, with lots of dead leaves, sticks, and some wild flowers trying valiantly to grow in the dry sunny area.

The first time we saw Tarsi dance, we did not know what he was doing. He began by picking up a stick in his beak and tossing it up in the air. Then he would flap his wings and begin to jump up and down. As he gained momentum, he would call out "carroo, carroo," and pick up more sticks and toss them high in the air.

Of course, we could not resist joining in the fun, and so it became a morning ritual to dance with Tarsi. Anyone who happened to get up early enough in the morning and visit the Ranger Station near the wildlife refuge was sure to see three little girls in flowered cotton nightgowns jumping up and down, flapping their arms like

wings, and throwing sticks up in the air with a three-foot tall grey-cinnamon crane with a wing-span of five feet. And all four of us would dance around in this crazy circle for about ten minutes, singing "carroo, carroo, carroo."

One morning, Dad happened to come home early from his daily bird scouting trip at dawn and catch us doing our morning dance ritual. He walked up to us laughing and said, "Do you know why Tarsi is dancing like that?"

"No," we yelled, stopping our dance to run towards him, "tell us!"

"Well, it's a habitual dance of all Greater Sandhill Cranes. They usually do it in the spring and summer months.

"But why do they dance?" I asked.

"Well, our research tells us they dance for a couple of reasons," answered Dad. "Sometimes we see them dance when they are alarmed or dis-turbed, but mainly they dance at sunrise and sunset in a type of celebration to show they feel good."

"Well, it certainly is fun," chimed in Michelle.

"Come into the house and I'll show you some pictures I have of the cranes dancing at sunset," said Dad.

So that morning, we all tromped back into the Ranger Station and sat at the kitchen table to look at colored photographs of cranes dancing. These were intense photographs, showing the large cranes in black silhouette against an orange-red sky. Dark marsh grasses and cattails rose in the foreground, emphasizing the long legs of the cranes as they leaped in the air, facing one another with their wings spread and beaks lifted to the twilight sky in call - frozen forever in that stance on the glossy paper of the photo.

After seeing the photograph of the wild cranes dancing, it was even more meaningful to watch Tarsi dance. We did not realize until later, that by dancing with him, we were imprinting him to the human way of life. To us the dancing

was a fun and beautiful game, and it became a
morning ritual to look forward to.

Another favorite ritual was the morning
walk. This usually took place after the morning
dance, or sometimes after breakfast.

Situated next to the Ranger Station were

the Grays Lake National Wildlife Refuge headquarters buildings. Beyond this was a lovely green
hill covered with wildflowers. It was the perfect
place to take a morning or evening walk.

Crossing the refuge headquarters did not
take long, so we were soon at the base of the hill
where we could begin slowly climbing towards the
summit. This generally took thirty minutes each
way and Tarsi would always accompany us - humming to himself as he happily hunted for grass-
hoppers and other insects among the flowers and

grasses.

The grasses were tall in places and we often got covered in wet dew to the waist, but we didn't mind because we were busy hunting for insects with Tarsi. To do this, we would scan the flowers; pink sticky geranium, red Indian paintbrush, magenta fireweed, golden mule-ear sunflowers, pale blue flax, and white daisies. Often we found orange lady-bugs and dusty moths, but mainly we found mosquitoes. Mosquitoes abounded in Grays Lake, and we were constantly slapping an arm or leg to prevent another bite. Tarsi, on the other hand, delighted in the mosquitoes, as they were a major mainstay in his diet.

The walk always ended on the summit of the hill where we could look across the valley and see the marsh as it stretched for miles, surrounded by the tall Caribou mountain range. In the middle of the marsh was a large island called Bear Island. The island was misnamed, because we never saw any bear on it. Instead it was inhabited by moose and mule-deer. The cranes also went on the island as well as the marsh.

After gazing across the valley and marsh for awhile, we would run back down the hill - dashing through the tall grass, laughing, and screaming - while Tarsi would flap his wings and follow as fast as he could on his long black legs. We'd arrive back at the Ranger Station out of breath, but ready to begin the day.

Another favorite activity during the long lazy days of summer was fishing. And in order to go fishing, we first had to hunt for worms. Worm-hunting soon turned out to be another special skill of Tarsi's. In fact he became better at worm-hunting than we did by the end of the summer.

The best place to find worms was in the ditch in front of the house. The ditch was bordered by our front fence with the tall spruce trees and the gravel road which passed in front of the house. The bottom of the ditch was usually filled with muddy water, and long horsetail plants,

grasses and weeds which grew near the water. Along the sides, however, were banks of soft green moss and rich brown earth. It was here that we found the worms.

Worm-hunting equipment included a large bucket and small hand shovels. Once we had retrieved these from the barn behind the house, we'd head out to the ditch, Tarsi right behind us.

Soon we would all be on hands and knees, digging our shovels into the rich brown earth, eyes scanning the soil for worms. Before long, the shovels would be forgotten, and we would dig in the dirt with hands and fingers.

"Ugh, my fingernails are full of dirt," cried Michelle.

"Oh, don't be a baby," replied Celeste.

"Hey, there's a worm," I said.

And soon we would all be pulling worms out of their dark home in the earth and placing them in the bucket. The bucket was filled with dirt also, so the worms would feel more comfortable once they were tossed in there.

"Tarsi just ate my worm!"

We glanced over and there was Tarsi, slurping a worm through his beak. Then immediately he poked his head in the soil and pulled out another worm.

"Hey, stop that," I yelled.

But Tarsi only moved a few steps away from us and continued to scan the ground looking for worms.

We soon discovered that his eye sight was much keener than ours, and to our dismay, Tarsi was able to sight and eat the worms faster than we could even begin to see them. His sharp brown eyes would dart back and forth across the surface, and then suddenly he would dart forward and pull another worm from the earth with his long black beak.

And so worm-hunting became another favorite ritual for Tarsi, even though he made it more challenging for us. He also made it more fun though, because it became a contest of who could find the most worms - Tarsi or us.

Even though Tarsi was superior at worm-hunting, he was not allowed to go fishing with us, where we would reap the benefits of having the

worms. When Dad came home in the evenings, Celeste and I would jump in the pickup truck, with our small fishing poles safely stored in the back. Michelle would stand outside with Mom, usually bawling because she was too small to go fishing.

Off we'd go, down the gravel road, a cloud of dust rising from behind the truck, as the sun slowly slid closer to the western horizon.

The fishing hole we most frequently used was near Gravel Creek campground. We'd stop along the road near the tall willow bushes, and then trek back into the dense brush along the creek. The going was difficult, as the willow bushes were thick and often would swing back and hit us in the face. There were many fallen aspen trees and shrubby undergrowth that also lay in wait to trip the unsuspecting.

After walking for about twenty minutes, we arrived at the beaver dam pond that was our fishing hole. By that time, our feet would be soaking

wet and cold, and the mosquitoes would be buzz-
ing in a halo around our heads. But this was all
part of the experience of fishing, as Dad told us.

And so, we grabbed our poles, checked
our bobbers, and then baited a worm on the
hook. Celeste and I cast our lines out across the
calm water and waited for the tell-tale tug on
the bobber. Dad usually used lures or feathery-
looking hooks, but we always used the worms that
Tarsi had helped us find.

The pond water at that time of evening
had a lovely molten silver sheen to it, with tiny
rivulets of pink, purple, and mauve reflected
from the dusky sky. Small insects danced across
the surface of the water, and the tall willows that
surrounded the pond were perfectly still in their
pale green leaves, as there was no breeze to rustle
the branches. Night sounds could be heard in
the distance - the call of an owl, the incessant
buzz of the mosquitoes, and occasionally, if we
were lucky, the loud slap of a beaver's tail as it hit

the water to warn its fellow family members that we were present. And then a large ripple would appear on the pond as the beaver dove deep under the water to find the underground passage to his lodge of sticks and mud.

"I think I've got one," I whispered excitedly, pointing at my red and white bobber jerking quickly on the water.

"Shhhh," said my father. "You'll scare the fish. Now reel it in slowly."

Hands shaking, I slowly reeled in my line, turning the handle on the fishing reel as steadily as I could. As more line was reeled in, I could feel the fish on the other end wiggling and diving as it tried to escape. At times it would seem as if the fish had slipped off the line, but Dad said he was just resting or playing with me. Finally, the line went completely taut, and I could feel the weight of the fish as I reeled it towards shore.

"Celeste, get the net," my father whispered.

Celeste jumped for the net and ran excitedly to the edge of the pond waiting to bag my fish as I pulled it out of the water.

And there he was - a beautiful twelve-inch Cutthroat trout. He flipped about in the net basket, and then Dad came forward to take him off the hook. I touched his moist slick skin, admiring the shimmering colors of silver, white, and red.

We strung the trout on a fish chain, and dropped it back into the water, attaching the end of the chain to the branch of a willow.

We continued to fish, as the lavender dusk slowly overtook the sky. We each caught a couple more fish, and those that were too small, we gently removed from the hook and placed back in the water where they swam away to safety.

"It's important," said my father, "to only take what you need from the wild. You should never be wasteful or destructive towards nature. Remember the wild animals only hunt for food - and that is a lesson from which we all can learn."

Celeste and I nodded our heads in agreement. Living so close to nature, it was easy to see how all animals and plants were necessary for the continued growth of one another.

We caught five more fish that evening that were large enough to take home. It was nearly dark, with the first evening stars visible in the sky, when Dad motioned it was time to leave. So we tramped back through the brush and water until we located the truck.

Back at the Ranger Station, Tarsi was waiting for us. He ran up to the truck door as we opened it and peered curiously inside to see what we had. As Dad pulled the fish out of the back of the truck, Tarsi ran forward to him and began to purr in excitement. Tarsi knew that the next ritual was cleaning the fish.

And sure enough, Dad would stand outside near the picnic table, cleaning the fish so we could cook them for dinner. But it was Tarsi's dinner too, because as fast as Dad would drop the fish scraps on the grass, Tarsi would swoop forward, grab them in his beak, and gobble them down. His brown eyes danced in the light from the back porch and he continued to purr and hum in delight, as he quickly downed the fish innards.

That night, as we all sat around the kitchen table next to the wood stove, Tarsi was too full and too tired to reach over Michelle's shoulder to sneak food from her plate. Instead he stood in a corner of the kitchen, one leg tucked up inside his feathers, his long neck and head looped around on his back in a gentle resting position, and went to sleep.

CHAPTER THREE

Visitors

Visitors to the Ranger Station were uncommon, since Grays Lake was located far from major roads and cities, but the valley people often stopped to visit. They were very friendly, usually bringing a newly canned jar of huckleberry jam or baked bread, and then staying to chat about the crops, the weather, the cattle, or the next church social.

Our favorite neighbor was Vera Call, because she always brought her children, two boys and a little girl to visit, so we had someone to play with.

The first time the Calls visited, in their blue Chevy four-door, Tarsi was already three feet tall. As the car drove slowly up our gravel driveway to stop near the side of the house, Tarsi stepped forward from behind a lilac bush to greet the visitors.

"Help," we heard a voice shouting, as we sat inside the house at the table drinking punch. "Help!"

We ran outside and there was Tarsi, trying to stick his long black beak in the car window. Vera was frantically rolling up the window, while still leaving enough space to call out so we could hear her from the house.

"Tarsi," we yelled. "Stop that."

Tarsi obediently moved over to where we stood on the sidewalk, then Mom went forward to help Vera out of the car.

"I thought it was going to attack my kids," breathed Vera heavily.

"I don't think he'll hurt you," answered Mom. "He's just not used to visitors and so he doesn't know how to respond. His name is Tarsi. He's a sandhill crane."

"I know he's crane," quipped Vera, "I grew up in this valley, but usually they stay in the marsh or out in the fields eating all our grain."

I stepped forward. "He's a pet. We raised him since he was only a few inches tall. Here, come closer and I'll introduce you."

But Vera refused to move closer to Tarsi, and it was a standstill until the door on the other side of the car opened and a small girl got out. Her name was Emmy and she slowly approached us and put her hand out towards Tarsi. Tarsi responded by gazing at her with his brown eyes and searching her palm for food.

"He's nice, Mommy," she said.

Slowly her brothers, Lance and Rusty, came forward, and Tarsi calmly accepted their presence, gazing at them with bright curious eyes. "He's so tall," said Rusty, the younger brother, turning to his mother to encourage her to move closer.

But just then Tarsi darted forward and, with his

beak, pulled forth the red bandana scarf that Rusty had in his back pocket. Before Rusty could turn around, Tarsi skipped away around the side of the house.

"He took my bandana," yelled Rusty, pointing after Tarsi.

Celeste, Michelle, and I immediately chased after Tarsi to retrieve the scarf, but he was too quick for us. He raced around the house on his long black legs, with grey wings flapping, and the red scarf trailing from his beak. As we approached him, he quickly turned at an angle, and was off again. Rusty, Lance, and Emmy joined in the chase, and soon it was a mad game of tag with Tarsi. We ran around the house in circles, shouting and laughing with fun.

At one point, Celeste was able to grab the scarf from Tarsi by hiding behind one of the lilac bushes, and then jumping out at him as he rounded the corner of the house, but he quickly got it back from her when she made the mistake of trailing it behind her. Finally, Tarsi tired of the game and dropped the bandana on the ground, so we easily retrieved it.

After that, whenever the Calls came to visit, Tarsi would greet them in the same manner by approaching their car and standing next to the car door daring them to get out. Vera never failed to call for help, so that we would rush out of the house to assist her past our fierce guard-crane, Tarsi.

Then all of us kids would play tag, and eventually this evolved into a great game of hide-and-seek. Tarsi was "it" and he had to find us. We would hide in the bushes or under the porch and wait and see if he could spot us. He almost always did, unless he got side-tracked by a dragon fly or some other insect that whizzed by his head and stole his attention from the game.

Towards the end of July, grandpa and grandma came to visit, as well as Uncle Tom and his Irish Setter dog, Mandy. Mandy was a large, red, nervous dog that had a habit of chewing up anything that was placed near her. She chewed up Tarsi's water bowl, popped our green rubber ball with her long white teeth, and devoured several pieces of laundry that Mom had hung out on the fence to dry. Within one day, Mandy had made serious enemies within our household. So we were quite delighted when Tarsi decided to teach Mandy a lesson.

That evening as we were gathered around the barbecue pit outside roasting hotdogs and hamburgers, Mandy came careening around the side of the house and screeched to a stop under the picnic table, quivering next to Uncle Tom's legs.

"What's wrong, Mandy?" he asked.

Mandy continued to shake and shiver under the table. Just then Tarsi stalked up, his brown eyes moving quickly back and forth amongst the gathered throng of people, searching for someone or something. Then in a lightening quick move, he darted forward and poked his beak under the table at Mandy.

"Arrfff," shrieked Mandy, as she jumped up

from under the table and raced across the yard.

"Carrooo," yodeled Tarsi, as he raced after her, wings flapping and long legs paddling the grass.

Then with precise aim, Tarsi sailed forward and pecked Mandy on the backside.

"Arrfff" shrieked Mandy again and then again as Tarsi continued his pursuit and attack to her backside.

Round and round, dog and crane ran in a crazy circle in the yard, until finally Mandy fled under the porch. Tarsi paced up and down in front of the porch, waiting for Mandy to come out, and he was still there pacing when we all went into the house to prepare for bed.

Uncle Tom eventually took pity on Mandy and shooed Tarsi away from the porch. He then had to crawl under the porch to coax Mandy out, as she was too unnerved to come out on her own.

The next day there was more ruckus, as we awoke to the sounds of blood-curdling shrieks coming from the vicinity of the outhouse. My father leaped from bed and ran outside, all of us fast on his heels.

"Heeeeellllppppp!" came the prolonged scream from the outhouse. "I'm trapped in here!"

There was Tarsi, guarding the door to the outhouse in his usual morning routine, and pecking his long black beak into the crack in the door. Unfortunately the person in the outhouse wasn't familiar with this friendly morning game.

"Heeellllppppp," came the long drawn-out scream again, and it sounded suspiciously like grandma.

My father moved forward to push Tarsi out of the way and then knock on the door. "Is that you Mother?"

"Oh, son, son, thank goodness. I thought I would die of a heart-attack in here."

The door to the outhouse slowly opened and out walked grandma, reaching forward to lean a hand heavily on Dad's shoulder.

"I've been in there for nearly one hour," she sighed.

Grandma had to spend the remainder of the day resting in bed, and Mom scolded us that we were not to teach Tarsi bad habits like the outhouse game anymore. But try as we might, we could not dissuade Tarsi from playing the morning outhouse game, and he trapped other visitors in the outhouse that summer and autumn as well.

Probably one of Tarsi's most colorful encounters with visitors occurred at Yellowstone Park.

Grandpa and grandma announced one morning during their visit that they really wanted to see Yellowstone. Since Grays Lake is located only twenty miles from the Wyoming border and it is only a two-hour drive to Yellowstone, we packed up a picnic, piled into the station wagon and started out.

"What about Tarsi?" I asked.

"He'll be fine by himself for one day," said my Dad. "We've left him alone before when you and Mom went into town to buy groceries."

"Yeh, but we'll be gone all day," chimed in Celeste. "We won't get back until late."

"Tarsi," wailed Michelle.

"Let's take him with us," suggested my grandfather.

To this statement, we all responded with loud cries of joy, with the exception of my father. Eventually his objections were overcome, and a cardboard box and blanket were arranged in the back of the station wagon, as well as small bowls of food for Tarsi.

Tarsi was amazingly well behaved on the drive to Yellowstone; sleeping in his box the majority of the time, or peering out the window and carrooing softly at the sights.

When we reached the town of Jackson Hole, we drove through to the first Yellowstone Visitor's Center. Dad agreed that we could let Tarsi out for a minute over near some trees, but then he had to go back in his box in the car while we went into the Visitor's Center.

Tarsi obligingly took care of his natural duties outside on the ground, and then wandered over to one of several small bubbling hot pools near the parking lot. These pools were part of the natural thermal springs that created the geysers throughout Yellowstone. Then before we could stop him, he put his foot in the water. Immedi-

ately he pulled it back out and shook it off as he realized how hot the water was.

"Ok, time to put him back in the car," Dad announced. "We don't want him to burn his feet."

Dad picked Tarsi up, but he carrooed loudly in protest when we put him back in his box in the car and left him there. We could see his head sticking up and peering out the window, his beak open wide as he called to us.

"He'll be fine," said Dad. So we went into the Visitor's Center.

It was a half an hour later while I was busily engaged in examining an exhibit of the geology of Yellowstone, that a woman ran into the Visitor's Center shrieking loudly, "There's an ostrich in the parking lot! An ostrich in the parking lot!"

People crowded forward to peer out the window as she pointed wildly towards the paved parking lot outside.

"Now ma'am, you must be mistaken," said a Park Ranger. "Ostriches are not native to Yellowstone."

"I tell you I saw one," she yelled. "Come on, I'll show you."

She stormed out the front door, a large crowd of people following her.

"Oh no," said my mother worriedly. And then she and my father dashed outside with the crowd.

Celeste, Michelle, and I followed to find a large circle of people surrounding our car. We pushed forward to the edge of the crowd and there in the middle of the pavement was my grandfather and Tarsi. Grandpa was proudly showing off Tarsi, pointing to his feathers and beak, speaking to the crowd like a trained wildlife expert.

"Yes, and you see," he said, "these birds are quite rare. He's a Greater Sandhill crane and will grow to be eight feet tall."

"No he won't grandpa," piped up Michelle in her high-pitched five-year old voice. "Greater

Sandhill cranes only grow to be about four to four and a half feet tall."

"What is this?" interrupted the Park Ranger, very official looking in his grey and green uniform with the badges. "You can't have cranes roaming around in the parking lot."

"Excuse me," my father said, moving forward. "I think I can explain the situation..."

And as the crowd gawked and pointed, Dad explained to the Park Ranger why a three-foot tall grey sandhill crane happened to be walking around a Visitor Center parking lot in Yellowstone.

On the ride home, grandpa was subjected to the back seat in disgrace.

"I still don't understand why you did that Pops?" said my Dad from the front seat as he drove towards home.

"Well I didn't see the harm in letting Tarsi out of the car for a few minutes. I went outside and could see him calling to me through the car window. Besides, he's a beautiful bird and ought to be showed off a little."

Sitting in the back seat next to grandpa, I slipped my hand into his hand and smiled up at him. I understood perfectly well why grandpa had let Tarsi out. Grandpa loved Tarsi has much as I did, and he wanted other people to see him so they would love him too.

CHAPTER FOUR

The Zoo Sojourn

Towards mid August Tarsi tried a few beginning attempts at flying. His most successful moments were during the morning walk ritual when we ran back down the hill. Since the hill was rather steep, Tarsi would stretch out his wings and sail for several yards through the air before landing on his feet. Then he would take another running start and fly a few more yards until, in this fashion, he reached the bottom of the hill.

It became difficult for us to keep up with Tarsi when we were all coming down the hill. For even though we held out our arms to the breeze and tried jumping forward in the air, we could not fly with him. Later in the week, we told Dad that Tarsi was learning how to fly.

Dad looked at us rather grimly. "Girls, I'm sorry to tell you, but we are going to have to clip Tarsi's wings so he won't fly."

"Why?" we chorused in dismay.

"Because even though he was born in the wild, he did not grow up in the wild and it might be unsafe for him to fly away from the house. An eagle or coyote could get him."

"But how will he migrate south in the winter time?" I asked.

"Right now we are making arrangements for Tarsi to spend the winter at the zoo in Pocatello, Idaho," Dad answered.

We knew the Pocatello Zoo was a nice place because we had visited there several time before. It was a place of lush green grass and tall shade trees with a lovely pond in the center. The animals were kept in large roomy areas surrounded by a fence, but it still seemed scary to leave Tarsi there all winter.

"You know he can't go back to the university

with us this winter. Where would he stay in our apartment?" asked Dad logically.

The University of Idaho was located in Moscow, and we had to return there in the winter so Dad could continue with his writing and classes. It was only during the summer and early autumn that we could live at Grays Lake.

"Will Tarsi get to come back next summer to live with us?" Michelle asked in a tearful voice.

"We hope so," responded Dad.

So Tarsi had his wings clipped later that week, and though he continued to try to fly, he could not go far. Instead he glided a few feet above the horse pasture near the barn, and still sailed down the hill a little in the mornings. Dad didn't clip his wings completely, because he said he wanted Tarsi to get the feel of flying so that someday we could return him to the wild.

September arrived in Grays Lake and the days became cooler. The clear air had a sharp bite to it in the mornings and evenings, and frost covered the ground. On the hills, the aspen trees cloaked themselves in a gown of gold coins that tinkled in the breezes, and patches of mountain maple flared flame-red amongst the evergreen of the firs and pines. Elk began to bugle on the mountain sides, and out in the marsh the cranes began preparing for their long flight south to Colorado, New Mexico, Arizona and old Mexico. They practiced for the trip by taking test flights in large flocks that spiraled upwards to the top of the sky, disappearing above the clouds so you could only hear their far away cry, before they dropped back into sight in a long U-shape to alight in a field to rest.

September also brought the yellow school bus to the front of the Ranger Station, and Celeste, Michelle and I piled in to go to the one-room school house at the south end of the valley.

Tarsi always walked us to the bus each morning, following behind as we traipsed down the gravel lane to the main road. The other kids on the bus pointed and laughed at first, but Emmy and Rusty stood up for Tarsi, and soon the rest of the kids became as fascinated by Tarsi as everyone else who came in contact with him.

Tarsi also met us at the end of the day when we returned home. We would jump off the bus and race with him back to the house, his long black legs pulling ahead of us as he propelled

himself forward with his wings. He often wanted to do the crane-dance when we came home, perhaps because we didn't have time to do it in the mornings anymore.

Autumn evenings were spend huddled next to the wood stove in the kitchen doing homework or reading a book. Tarsi would stay near us, standing on one leg in the corner, his feathers ruffled for warmth. And high over the house, we could hear the wild cranes call as they prepared

for migration - practicing and testing their wing strength.

It was in early October that they finally left. Great masses of long grey birds swirling higher and higher up to the clouds, then forming permanent U-shaped flight formations that would take them south over one thousand miles to their winter marshes.

"The majority of the cranes migrate south along the crest of the Rocky Mountains, and then stop in the San Luis Valley of south-central Colorado," said Dad. "They rest for about a month at Monte Vista National Wildlife Refuge or in nearby fields. Then most head further south to winter at the Bosque del Apache National Wildlife Refuge in New Mexico, along the banks of the Rio Grande River."

"Why can't we follow them?" asked Celeste.

"I probably will as part of my banding studies," said Dad. "But you all need to go back to Moscow and go to school there this winter."

So the day came when Tarsi had to go to the Pocatello Zoo. It was a beautiful day - the type the valley folks called an "Indian Summer Day." It had snowed a little the week before, but today the sky was an intense blue, the air sharp and clear so that every tree and plant stood out in sharp relief, and the breeze felt warm and golden.

We all piled into the station wagon with Tarsi in the far back and the three of us in the back seat so that we could be near him. Mom and Dad sat in the front.

"Will the people at the zoo be nice to Tarsi?" asked Michelle.

"Yes, they will take good care of him there," said Mom.

The two hour ride seemed to go too fast, perhaps because we did not want it to end. But before we knew it we were driving into the zoo parking lot and the zoo keeper came out to the car to greet us.

"Welcome," he said with a big smile for all

Vivian Olsen

70

of us. "My name is Demar Day, and I'd like to thank you for letting me take care of Tarsi for you this winter."

He seemed very nice and we sighed with relief, as we petted Tarsi gently from the back seat. Dad went off with Demar for awhile, then they came back and we all got out of the car. Tarsi was placed in a temporary cage to be transported to his aviary.

The aviary in which Tarsi was placed was large and lovely. It looked more like a park with lots of grass, trees, and a pond. It was surrounded on all sides by a large wire-mesh fence, but there were other birds, including ducks and geese, so Tarsi wouldn't be lonely.

As we stood outside the fence, Demar took Tarsi's cage inside, then carefully opened the door to the cage. Tarsi stepped out and walked around tentatively. He poked his beak at the ground, then lifted his head towards the sky as if smelling the air. Demar placed a handful of grain on the ground, and Tarsi immediately began to eat it.

"I think he'll be fine," said Demar as he left the enclosure and walked back to us.

"Oh look," Celeste pointed excitedly towards Tarsi, "he's meeting some new bird friends."

We watched as several small ducks and a few Canada geese approached where Tarsi stood eating the grain. Tarsi lifted his head to look at them curiously as they began to eat, then returned to eating as well.

"Come on girls, it's time to go," my mother gently prompted. "Say good-bye to Tarsi."

"Bye Tarsi," I said. "See you next summer."

"Good-bye Tarsi," said Celeste.

"Bye, bye," sobbed Michelle, big fat tears running down her cheeks. "I'll miss you."

Mom put her arm around Michelle as we walked away. I felt like crying too, but since I was the oldest, I knew I shouldn't. Instead I gulped back the tears and smiled bravely. The end of summer had come and gone, and like the wild cranes, it was time for us to migrate as well. We would return again next summer to pick up Tarsi.

CHAPTER FIVE

Return to the Wild

"And you should have heard this lady yell.
Why she screeched like an angry goose when Tarsi
poked her in the backside."

Demar, the zoo keeper, laughed and
slapped his hands on his thighs in merriment as
he regaled us with stories of Tarsi's winter sojourn
at the zoo.

"But Tarsi didn't hurt her, did he?" asked
my Mother in concern.

"Oh no, he just startled her," replied
Demar. "We have signs that warn people not to
get too close to the fence, but this lady was appar-
ently leaning back against the fence eating a sand-
wich. She was very much overweight and wear-
ing a bright flowered dress and I guess Tarsi just

75

couldn't resist poking one of the flowers. Ha Ha! Ha!" Demar threw back his head again in laughter, and soon we all joined in. The picture he painted of Tarsi innocently poking the lady and sending her screaming to the zoo keeper's office was just too funny to resist.

"Don't get me wrong," said Demar. "I wouldn't laugh if it had been serious. But she didn't get hurt and in fact, once she got over her surprise, I took her back to visit Tarsi and told her all about him. She now brings her grandchildren to visit once a month and tells them about her encounter with Tarsi."

We smiled at this tale of Tarsi's adventures in the zoo. It sounded just like something Tarsi would do.

It was finally late spring again and we had returned to the Pocatello zoo to pick up Tarsi. The zoo keeper, Demar, welcomed us warmly and reassured us that Tarsi was fine. After offering us a soda in his office and telling us stories of Tarsi, we walked out to see him in the aviary.

"He's so much bigger," exclaimed Celeste when she first saw him.

And she was right. Tarsi looked like an adult Greater Sandhill Crane now. He stood over four feet tall and all of his feathers were a glossy silver grey. His eyes had lightened from brown to a piercing orange-yellow, and his beak and legs were shiny black. The most amazing thing about him though was the red marking on his head. This red cap of skin on top of the head and his yellow eyes were the marking of all adult sandhill cranes. He looked proud, imperious, and very beautiful.

"Tarsi," shrieked Michelle, as she ran towards the fence. "Tarsi."

"Now wait a minute Michelle," said my father as he reached for her hand. "It's been awhile since Tarsi has seen us. He may not remember us right away, since so many people have visited him this winter. We have to give him time."

"Tarsi," Michelle pouted and pushed my Dad's hand away. "Tarsi," she continued to call.

Celeste and I moved towards the fence and joined Michelle in her calling. At first Tarsi didn't pay any attention to us, and even walked away towards some trees.

"Tarsi, Tarsi," we continued to call.

Suddenly he cocked his head to the side and stopped walking. Then slowly he turned around and came towards us, continuing to tilt his head sideways as if he was listening to our voices.

"Tarsi, Tarsi," we called again and poked our fingers through the fence.

"Now, girls," cautioned my mother. "You know you are not suppose to put your fingers through the fence."

Tarsi had now reached the part of the fence where we stood. He stopped several feet from us and peered imperiously at us with his orange-yellow eyes. He seemed so tall and proud.

"Do you think he remembers us?" whispered Celeste.

"It appears so," said Demar happily, "but since he has been around so many people this past winter, you need to approach him slowly and gently when you get back home."

And so Tarsi came back to Grays Lake with us for another summer. As soon as he was released from his cage in the back of the station wagon, he strutted around the Ranger Station yard as if reclaiming it for his own. He approached the red pump and poked at it with his beak, then helped himself to a drink of water from a pan near the pump, lifting his head towards the sky, so the water could trickle back down his throat and long neck. He investigated the spruce trees and lilac bushes and then wandered around to the front of the house, looking quickly from side to side as if assessing his territory.

"I think he remembers," said Mom, "but give him time to get used to it again. Don't approach him too quickly and be careful of his beak. He could accidently hurt you."

So we slowly followed Tarsi around the yard, but didn't get too close to him, because as Mom and Dad said, it had been awhile since he had seen us and he needed time to get used to his surroundings again. He seemed content to explore the yard, and since his wings were still clipped, we knew he could not fly away.

That night Tarsi stayed outside and when we awoke in the morning, a thin layer of snow coated the ground. It was not uncommon for it to snow in May and early June at Grays Lake, since the altitude was above six thousand feet high.

We ran outside to see how Tarsi had fared the cold weather and found him huddled on the back porch next to the screen door, his grey feathers fluffed around him to ward off the cold.

"Can Tarsi come in the house Mom?" Celeste yelled over her shoulder from where she stood next to the back screen door. "He seems cold."

"Sure," said Mom, walking forward to look out the window with us.

We opened the door and gestured Tarsi inside, but he immediately hopped off the porch

steps and walked over to the spruce trees.

"He doesn't seem comfortable with us yet, girls," Mom said. "Just give him time."

And so we spent the remainder of the morning playing in the snow and keeping an eye out for Tarsi. He watched us from a distance, but whenever we came too close to him, he walked a few steps away from us. But Tarsi was more aware of us than we realized, as we discovered later that afternoon.

After a quick lunch of a steaming bowl of tomato soup, we spent another hour coloring in our color books, and then donned our snow clothes to go outside to build a snowman.

"Let's go over by the pond to build the snowman," said Celeste. "The snow looks fresher there."

The pond was located in the horse pasture next to the Ranger Station, but we had to go through a gate in the wooden pole fence to get there. We decided to leave the gate open behind us since there were no horses in the pasture, and we wanted to see if Tarsi would follow us. But he remained behind, guarding his post near the spruce trees.

The snow near the pond was undisturbed and of a perfect consistency to make snowballs and to build a snowman. I bent down in the snow and began to form a small snowball which I pushed along the ground until it grew larger.

"Come and help me push this," I shouted to Celeste and Michelle.

"Hey, there's ice on the pond," said Michelle excitedly.

I looked up to see Michelle and Celeste near the edge of the pond. Michelle was bending over to touch the ice with her gloves. I stopped my snowball rolling effort and walked over to join them.

"I wonder if it is hard enough to walk on," mused Celeste.

"I doubt it," I said. "Come on, we shouldn't

be near the pond anyway. You know Mom always says we should stay away from it. Let's build a snowman."

Celeste and Michelle followed me back to where I was beginning to roll the snowman, and together we pushed the ball until it grew quite large.

"There, that will make a perfect base," I said. "Let's start on the next snowball for the middle. We'll make a three tier snowman."

"I'm going to hunt for rocks for his eyes," announced Michelle in her five-year old voice.

"OK," we mumbled, not paying much attention, and Celeste and I went back to rolling the snowball.

Suddenly we were startled from our efforts by a loud trumpeting noise.

"Carrooooooooo, Carrooooooooo."

Looking up quickly we were amazed to see Tarsi standing near the edge of the pond flapping his large wings and yodeling loudly in a voice which was much deeper in tone that we had ever heard before. He continued to yell and jump about excitedly, and suddenly we saw a splashing in the pond near his feet.

Celeste and I left our snowball and ran over to the edge of the pond to see what it was.

"Oh, my gosh, it's Michelle," I screamed. "Go get Mom."

But Mom was already running across the pasture towards us, shouting for me to help Michelle. I dropped down on my hands and knees and reached for her hand. She was only in a couple of feet of water, but she appeared to be in shock because her face was white and she wasn't yelling.

Just then Mom reached us and together we pulled Michelle back onto the hard ground of the shore.

"What were you doing near the pond?" yelled Mom. She was very angry and her voice was shaking. "I always tell you not to play near the pond!"

Michelle began whimpering now and big icy tears ran down her cold cheeks. "I was trying to see if the ice was hard enough to skate on."

"Well it's not, and if Tarsi hadn't started yodeling like that I wouldn't have heard you from the house," said Mom. "Let's go back now so you can get warm."

Celeste and I glanced over at Tarsi. He still stood a little distant from us, but he was quiet now and gazed at the four of us with golden eyes.

"Thanks, Tarsi," I whispered. "You saved Michelle."

He gazed calmly back at us, not realizing what a hero he really was, and then slowly followed us back to the house.

After that first day when Tarsi saved Michelle from the icy pond, he seemed more at ease with us. As each day passed, he came closer when we played outside, and by the end of the week, he let us pet his silvery-grey back feathers again.

Mom was incredibly grateful to Tarsi and told my father about how he had alerted us when Michelle was in the pond. Dad recorded the incident in his scientific notes and agreed with us that Tarsi was a hero. Michelle had to stay in bed with a cold, but she was thankful to Tarsi as well and had learned her lesson about getting too close to the pond. As for Celeste and I, we were scolded for not keeping a closer eye on her.

But by early June, all was forgotten when Dad brought home three new baby Greater Sandhill cranes.

"Wow, three new cranes!" I shouted with excitement. "Are we going to raise them too, like Tarsi?"

"Yes, the wildlife people are trying to re-introduce Greater Sandhills to a refuge in Utah," responded Dad. "We are going to raise them for awhile, and then send them to the refuge later in the summer."

"But won't the babies miss their parents?" asked Michelle.

My father rubbed his chin thoughtfully at us, then smiled. "Sit down girls and let me explain to you how crane families develop. You see, each pair of parent cranes usually has two eggs. In the wild, one baby chick is usually stronger than the other. The stronger baby chick eats most of the food, and the weaker baby chick sometimes dies."

"But that's awful," exclaimed Michelle.

"It may seem awful to us," responded Dad, "but it is a natural event in the crane world. Only the strongest animals survive. This enables the species to continue. So you see, the baby chicks I bring home are the ones that might die anyway if we left them in the marsh. The other ones, left with their parents, will receive all the attention and will be well-fed."

"Was Tarsi one of the weaker chicks too?" I asked.

"Tarsi was actually lost when I found him," said Dad. "So I'm not sure, but it doesn't matter, because if given a chance both babies can live and grow strong. There are a few crane parents that managed to raise both chicks, but this is not common."

"So what will we name the new baby

cranes?" asked Celeste.

"It's up to you," smiled Dad. "But remember, later in the summer, they will go to live at the refuge and will not come back again."

"What about Tarsi?" I asked.

"Tarsi will stay with us this summer and return to the zoo again in the winter."

And so we had three new baby sandhill cranes to watch and take care of. We eventually named them Tibby, Tuffy, and Tilly, attempting

to keep the first letter of each name a "T" like
Tarsi.

The baby cranes grew fast, just as Tarsi had.
We were concerned that Tarsi would be jealous of
them, but he just appeared mildly curious. The
first few weeks the babies stayed inside so Tarsi
didn't see them anyway, but by mid-June, we arranged for cages to be set-up in the yard so they
could enjoy the sun.

Tarsi wandered over to the cages and peered
at them, and then wandered off to eat insects. We
still played our morning rituals with Tarsi each
day - doing the outhouse run, dancing with him,
and taking the morning walk up the hill. He easily
fell back into all of the rituals after the first week
of returning home.

He also enjoyed worm-hunting just as
much as he used to, and he still scared the Calls
and other visitors when they stopped by the
Ranger Station.

As the baby cranes grew, Tarsi appeared

to take more interest in them. By mid-summer he was playing crane hide-and-seek and tag with them, and soon they were large enough to learn the crane dance and join us in the mornings. But Dad said we were not to dance with the new cranes, because of the scientific theory of imprinting. He said that they should only dance with other cranes.

This was confusing to us, but we could still dance with Tarsi. And Tarsi remained our favorite, because he was our first crane, and closest to our hearts. Also, as an adult crane, he was the most impressive to look at, and he seemed to know it as he strutted around the yard and preened himself.

Tibby, Tuffy, and Tilly grew rapidly and when they began to stretch their wings and make attempts to fly, we ran and told Dad as we had when Tarsi first learned how to fly. But this time Dad did not clip their wings.

"But why not," I asked. "You clipped Tarsi's

wings when he was their age."

"Yes, but Tibby, Tuffy, and Tilly are going to the refuge later this summer. Tarsi is not. It is important that they learn how to fly now."

So the three new cranes practiced flying and soon they were able to glide over the horse pasture and towards the marsh. They always returned to the Ranger Station, but as the days passed, their wings grew stronger and they were able to fly further from the house.

For Tarsi this was very distressful. He tried

to fly with the other cranes, but could only glide a few yards and then land on the ground. He cried out in frustration, yodeling at the top of his voice and strutting angrily around in a circle, all the while glaring at the sky where the other cranes flew.

We told Dad that we thought this was not fair to Tarsi, but he said we were doing it for Tarsi's own good. "Tarsi might get hurt, because he's not used to the wild. Tibby, Tuffy, and Tilly are not domesticated like Tarsi."

And so we had to watch Tarsi's frustration and tried to sooth him as best we could with games and food. One day he did manage to fly with the other cranes further than usual, and landed in a cow pasture down the road. He was unable to muster enough wing power to fly over the fence and out of the pasture, so Mom and Dad had to go rescue him and bring him home in the station wagon.

He came home gratefully and immediately lay claim to the house and yard as his territory. Even though he could not fly off with the others, he was still king of his own yard, and was the dominant crane over the others when they were there.

The summer days passed swiftly and happily, and before we knew it, autumn had once again claimed Grays Lake in its golden wreath and it was time for the three young cranes to go to the

Utah refuge. Dad drove them there himself and returned to tell us that they were safely settled.

Tarsi appeared to miss them a little, but not much. He was once again the only one who received all of our attention and he seemed to enjoy this. But a month later, it was time for him to go to the Pocatello zoo for the winter and for us to return to Moscow. It was then that we realized that the migration cycle of the cranes had become our cycle, for our lives became scheduled around their return and departure from Grays Lake.

When we picked Tarsi up again the next spring, we were all very happy to be with him again in Grays Lake. It felt so right to return to the valley as the green shoots were bursting from the earth and the leaves and flowers were opening to the sun. The wild Greater Sandhill cranes conducted

their mating dance in the marsh and the cycle of birth and renewal began again.

The third summer with Tarsi was filled with more golden memories. He continued to amuse and delight us in his many little ways, and he still enjoyed participating in all the daily rituals.

Dad brought home five new baby cranes to raise that summer, and this time, when they began to learn how to fly, Tarsi was allowed to fly with them.

"But why?" we asked.

"Because we now believe that Tarsi will be able to return to the wild at the refuge in Utah as well," answered Dad. "They have an enclosed area where the cranes are carefully watched until the biologists there feel comfortable that the cranes can live safely and productively in the wild."

So at the end of that third summer together, Tarsi returned to the wild. The last few weeks with him were bittersweet as we watched him fly off with the new cranes and return in the late afternoons as the sun was sinking towards the marsh.

He still came to stand by us each evening as we sat on the front porch to watch the orange, red, and purple streaks paint the western sky and listen to the nightly orchestra of wild cranes calling in the marsh. Tarsi would stand calmly, softly humming to himself and eating mosquitoes, and it was this way I still remember him.

For whenever I see a glowing sunset and hear the wild cranes call, I feel Tarsi standing there beside me in all his quirky, amusing, delightful, and beautiful presence. And when I see a flock of wild cranes silhouetted against an evening sky, I envision him there among them, flying free and happy, and perhaps still playing a game of tag - but this time with another crane.

Some Interesting Facts About Greater Sandhill Cranes

By Dr. Rod Drewien

After studying and banding over 1,000 Greater Sandhill Cranes in the Grays Lake area, as wildlife biologists we have confirmed the following facts:

Young cranes remained with their parents in family units for the first 9-10 months of life and they learned the migration route by accompanying their parents. In future winters these younger birds normally returned to the same areas they had visited with their parents. They also continued to follow the same fall and spring migration routes and used the same stopover areas they had frequented with their parents. In this manner, migration traditions are passed down from generation to generation.

Young cranes started forming pairs at 2-4 year of age and first nested when 3-6 years old.

Family members, including offspring, continued to "recognize" each other over many years and temporarily joined together in extended family groups when they encountered each other during various periods in an annual cycle. Some marked siblings associated with each other up to 20 years after hatching.

Many banded cranes lived for 20-29 years, and a handful survived for 30-40 years. Their maximum life span in the wild, however, remains unknown.

The primary wintering area for the Rocky Mountain Population of Greater Sandhill Cranes is in Socorro and Valencia Counties in west-central New Mexico's Middle Rio Grande Valley. The most important winter concentration locations are the Bosque del Apache National Wildlife Refuge and the Ladd S. Gordon State Wildlife Management Areas near Belen, Casa Colorada, and Bernardo. Others winter at various locations in southwestern New Mexico, southeastern Arizona, and in the northern Mexican states of Chihuahua and Durango.

Important spring-fall migration stopover areas include but are not limited to the San Luis Valley, Colorado, the Colorado and Gunnison Valleys in western Colorado including Harts Basin, and in the Green River Valley near Jensen, in eastern Utah.

Positive Conservation Practices Have Helped to Save the Greater Sandhill Crane, But Continued Efforts Are Needed

Greater Sandhill Cranes of the Rocky Mountain Population were much reduced in numbers with settlement of the region during the 1870s-1930s. By the early 1940s up to 250 breeding pairs were estimated to remain in the entire region. The "subspecies" was classified as "Rare" by the U. S. Department of the Interior in 1966 with estimates of 6,000 remaining in North America; 2,000 east of and 4,000 west of the Rocky Mountains.

In 1968, researchers in Oregon estimated 10,000 in North America. By 1970, we estimated some 10,000 in the Rocky Mountain Population alone and they were removed from their "Rare" classification. Good conservation practices including improved protection from illegal shooting, expansion of favorable agricultural practices, and the establishment of state and federal refuges and wildlife management areas throughout the region have contributed much to their increases in numbers.

By 2007-2009, the Rocky Mountain Population had doubled to 20,000-23,000. This population is currently reoccupying much of its historic nesting ranges in Colorado, Idaho, Montana, Utah, Wyoming and northward into Alberta, Canada. Maintaining and protecting sufficient wintering habitat is the most important management need for the long-term welfare of this Population. Many wetland and riparian habitats in the arid southwestern United States and northern Mexico have been modified or lost to development and their future status will be dependent upon winter habitat protection and favorable management practices.

Seasonal distribution of the Rocky Mountain Greater Sandhill Crane Population nesting at Grays Lake, Idaho. The Grays Lake cranes migrate through northeastern Utah and southwestern Wyoming to the San Luis Valley in southcentral Colorado. They winter mainly in the Middle Rio Grande Valley, New Mexico, and follow the same route northward in spring.

The Forest Service Ranger Station, located next to the Grays Lake National Wildlife Refuge, where our family lived with Tarsi.

Tarsi, as a baby, in the first few days after his adoption.

Liz (author) and Michelle each holding two baby Sandhill Cranes.

Research Biologist Dr. Rod Drewien and Tarsi near the end of the first summer. Tarsi is nearly a full-grown Sandhill.

About the Author

Liz Drewien Thach is a professional writer and business professor. Growing up in Idaho, she developed a great love for the outdoors, and her book, *Tarsi, The Sandhill Crane*, describes what it was like living so close to wildlife. Now with a Ph.D. in Human Resource Development, Liz lives in California and teaches full-time at Sonoma State University. In her free time, she focuses on a new passion of grape-growing and winemaking. This experience feeds into her four wine business textbooks, published under her professional name of Dr. Liz Thach (pronounced "tosh".) In addition, she enjoys writing mystery novels with her good friend, Kathleen Kelly. Together they publish under the pen name of Kathleen Tosh, and have created the intriguing Lia Jordan Wine Travel Mystery Series, featuring *Chardonnay Chalice*, and the Cassandra Aragon B&B Suspense Series. Liz can be reached at *http://www. kathleentoshbooks.wordpresss.com*

Liz's father, the wildlife biologist featured in *Tarsi, the Sandhill Crane*, is now retired and lives in Grays Lake during the summer. Her mother became a famous artist specializing in wildlife, and created the drawings in this book, as well as the painting used for the front cover. Her little sister Michelle is a professional graphic designer living in Seattle and completed the design for this book.

About the Artist

Vivian C. Olsen paints birds and animals as she experiences them in the wild - inhabitants of the places she loves to explore. She began painting and drawing as a child and studied art in college – achieving both a B.A. in General Studies and M.A. in Science Teaching. She has worked as a wildlife illustrator, an art educator at the high school level in New Mexico, and as a professional artist exhibiting and selling her paintings throughout the nation. Vivian is an active member of the High Desert Art League, Plein Air Painters of Oregon, Oil Painters of America, and ArtWise. Her paintings can be found at *http://www.vivianolsen.com*.

About the Book Designer

Michelle Drewien (the same Michelle in the book who Tarsi rescued from the pond) is now President and Creative Director of Zango Creative in Seattle, Washington. She received a B.F.A. in Graphic Design from the University of Idaho, and established her very successful company in 1996. Her clients range from Fortune 500 companies to the business next door. Zango Creative specializes in web and print design and includes a team of highly experienced design, technology, writing and marketing professionals. For more information, see *http://www.zangocreative.com*.

About Grays Lake National Wildlife Refuge, Wayan, Idaho

Established in 1965, Grays Lake National Wildlife Refuge is composed of 19,400 acres and is the largest hardstem bulrush marsh in the US. It is surrounded by high mountains, with the tallest peak, Caribou Mountain, reaching 9803 feet. It is located in southeastern Idaho, 27 miles from Soda Springs and only 19 miles from the Wyoming border.

Even though it is called Grays "Lake," it doesn't have much water, but is a perfect marsh for over 200 species of wild birds, fish and other animals. It is most famous for its very large population of Greater Sandhill Cranes, with as many as 1200 being counted at one time. The rare trumpeter swan can also be found at Grays Lake. The whole valley is still breathtakingly beautiful and quite pristine and unspoiled – a part of America that few people visit. See _http://www.fws.gov/grayslake_.

Made in the USA
Charleston, SC
02 December 2011